The World of the
INDIA

The World of
INDIA

Text and photographs
by Henri Stierlin

SUNFLOWER BOOKS,
MAYFLOWER BOOKS, INC.,
575 LEXINGTON AVENUE,
NEW YORK CITY 10022.

A PRODUCTION OF AGENCE INTERNATIONALE D'ÉDITION JEAN F. GONTHIER
8, Ave. Villardin, 1009 Pully (Switzerland)

End papers

The façades of the Kandarya Mahadeo temple at Khajuraho are adorned with admirable sculptural carvings representing apsaras (heavenly nymphs) and deities. The crowd of gods here seen at the base of the lofty spire crowning the edifice ressembles the multitude of saints on a cathedral porch. These sculptures dating from the eleventh century are the most sublime expression of medieval art in India.

Title page

This marvellous Buddha carved in red sandstone dates from the Gupta period (Fifth century A.D.). It ranks among the masterpieces of Buddhist sculpture in India. The halfclosed eyes and pure and serene features reflect the profound meditation of the Enlightened One. (Museum of Mathura)

ISBN 08317-9611-1
Printed in Italy by Lego

Contents

From the Origins to Buddhism

Facing page :
Monumental Buddhist sculpture first appears about 25 A.D. at Sanchi in central India. This yakshi, or tree-nymph, symbol of the fecund energy of nature, decorates the eastern gate of the Great Stupa.

Below :
These two stupas at Sanchi dating back to the first and third centuries B.C. mark the birth of Buddhist architecture in India. The dome-like structures symbolize the Buddha's tomb and often contain relics of the Merciful One.

Detail of one of the carved pillars decorating the toranas, or gates, at Sanchi : these low reliefs depict scenes from the life of the Buddha who is himself never represented. The procession portrays Gautama's Great Departure.

To the eyes of the western reader, the world of India represents exotic climates, a lavish pageant of religions worshipping multiple divinities, the complexity of a society governed by a system of countless castes, the infinite diversity accompanying intricately intertwined civilizations... India calls to mind a forest of temples bristling with sculptural carvings, the maharajahs' sumptuous palaces, gods equipped with numerous pairs of gesticulating arms, elephant armies, etc.

But India is also the cradle of an art expressive of mankind's loftiest spiritual yearnings, a site that has given birth to monuments extolling the purity of meditation and self-denial, enlivened by the soaring ideals of an irrepressible faith.

The Setting

India is often called a subcontinent : indeed, this vast peninsula jutting into the Indian Ocean like a wedge between the Arabian sea and the Bay of Bengal is cut off from the rest of Asia by the Himalayas and may consequently be considered as a distinct entity. It is separated from the main body of the continent on the north-west by the deserts of Baluchistan and the Hindu Kush and on the north-east by the Burmese mountains. The Khyber pass in present day Afghanistan commands access to the country. It was the gateway to India for the waves of invaders which successively swept over this immense territory, as large as the whole of Western Europe.

South of the mountains are two wide fertile plains, watered on the

The Great Stupa at Sanchi is surrounded by high stone barriers which mark the bounds of the area reserved for the rite of circumambulation. It was begun in the third century B.C. The Toranas, decorated with sculptural carvings, were added at the beginning of the first century A.D.

Right :
A stone portico remarkable for its purity of line is all that now remains of Stupa XVIII at Sanchi where the followers of the Buddha came together for religious ceremonies.

west by the Indus, in modern Pakistan, and on the east by the Ganges, the delta of which is now the State of Bangladesh. They are the subcontinent's richest and most densely populated areas. The Deccan, a triangular tableland bounded by the Eastern and Western Ghats, covers the southern portion of India. The country has a tropical monsoon climate. The Indian year may be divided into two seasons, one extremely rainy and the other one dry.

This setting characterized by violent contrasts and, in many regions, by a luxuriant vegetation, witnesses the successive development of the great Indian civilizations, the origins of which date back to the dawn of history and the third millenium B.C.

A Compelling Choice

We should, in vain, endeavour to evoke here more than 4000 years of history and mention the hundreds of sites and thousands of masterpieces scattered over this truly cultural continent. In order to give an account of the art and civilization of India as comprised within its present boundaries, we can but choose from representative monuments and works of art. This choice, centred on a very limited number of exceptional achievements, will allow us in addition to study the important periods all the more thoroughly. Our aim is to deal with each fundamental style, each great artistic trend. A certain diffuseness would indeed be unavoidable if we were to take into account the all too profuse variants.

In order to better define our intentions and in particular the directing principle that has motivated our choice, we shall begin with an outline of the itinerary of this trip through time on which we invite our readers. As regards the Buddhist period, the first to have left significant vestiges in India, we evoke the stupas at Sanchi (third century B.C. — first century A.D.) and the cave temples at Ajanta (second century B.C. — seventh century A.D.). The masterpieces of Buddhist sculpture — among others the classical creations which flourished at Mathura (fourth and fifth centuries) — were produced during the Gupta period.

Below :
The generalized and simplified capitals in the Buddhist temple at Sanchi betray a remote influence of Achaemenid Persian architecture. The columns raised by King Asoka in the third century B.C. are also derived from Iran.

The monumental stone railings surrounding the stupas are merely enlarged copies of primitive log fences.

Sacred enclosure surrounding the Great Stupa at Sanchi: a stairway leads to the upper level where the rite of circumambulation was performed on a raised circular platform following the side of the main structure.

Above right:
Detail of a sculptured panel adorning a gate pillar at Sanchi. We may distinguish, among groups of winged griffons, the great symbols of the Buddhist faith: above, the hemispherical stupa surrounded by a fence and meant to represent the tomb of the Buddha; in the centre, the Wheel of preaching, or Dharma, which refers to the doctrine of the Merciful One.

The caves and rock-cut temples at Ellora furnish a transition from the Buddhist and Jain world to the Hindu renaissance which begins in southern India in the seventh and eighth centuries with the sanctuaries carved out of granite along the shore at Mamallapuram. Another art which flourished in the south was bronze sculpture which reached a peak of perfection in the tenth century under the Chola dynasty.

We return to the Gangetic plain to evoke the great sanctuaries of the Medieval period, in particular the famous temples at Khajuraho, dating from the tenth and eleventh centuries, and the admirable sculptural carvings, sometimes described as erotic, which decorate their façades. Hinduism, faced with the onslaught of the Muslim invaders, succeeds in maintaining its independence only in the south where tremendous temple complexes are erected, as for example the one built at Madura in the seventeenth century.

The Muslim invasions and the conquest of northern India by Islam mark a sudden break in the modes of artistic expression. The first monument raised by the Muslim conquerors, who establish their capital at Delhi, is the Qutb Minar and the Quwwat al-Islam mosque dating from the early thirteenth century. The fortress at Daulatabad is one of the most fantastic citadels erected by the Muslims in the sixteenth century on the ruins of a Hindu stronghold. The Mogul empire leaves such vestiges as the tomb of Humayun (1565) and the famous Red Fort at Delhi. During the reign of Akbar the Great we witness the construction of the city of Fatehpur Sikri (1570) and the palaces of the Red Fort at Agra which is also the site of a series of extravagant tombs culminating in the Taj Mahal (seventeenth century).

In the service of the Great Moguls, the Rajput maharajahs have brought the region of Jaipur to a pinnacle of wealth and power well attested by the palace at Amber and the astronomical observatory erected by Jai Singh II in the eighteenth century.

Such is the choice we deem most appropriate. It includes essentially

Eastern gate, or torana, of the Great Stupa at Sanchi. The low reliefs decorating the architraves depict Asoka's visit to the bodhi tree in the shade of which the Buddha mediated; Sakyamuni's departure for his long march towards truth; and, at the summit, the Seven Last Buddhas symbolized by vacant thrones.

Left:
Detail of the Temptation of Buddha: this low relief decorating the middle architrave of the northern torana of the Great Stupa at Sanchi depicts a group of grimacing and gesticulating demons trying to disturb the Buddha's meditation.

11

Stupa III at Sanchi, dating from the first century B.C., has but one platform for the rite of circumambulation. The ashlar work encasing the dome-like structure is bulkier than that of the Great Stupa. At the summit, a stone copy of the umbrella which shaded the Buddha's meditation.

Right:
The inner face of the middle architrave of the eastern gate represents the dream of Maya, mother of the future Buddha, approached by a Bodhisattva riding a white elephant.

Facing page:
The first images of the Buddha appear about the second century A.D. and are the work of sculptors in the Gandhara province. This art, characterized by a distinct classical influence deriving from Hellenistic sources, is called Greco-Buddhist. The purity of the features, the elegance of the half-closed eyes, the unbroken line joining the eyebrows and the bridge of the nose, the hair arranged in large loose curls are typical of this stucco sculpture dating from the third century. (Museum of Delhi)

sites situated on a line cutting across India from north to south, disregarding as irrelevant to our purpose the far western region and the east coast of the peninsula as well as the foothills of the Himalayas. While this selection unquestionably reflects the author's own preferences, it is nonetheless representative and revealing of India's great artistic trends.

The Aryans and the Vedic Religion

When Buddha begins to preach, about 525 B.C., Indian civilization has already experienced long and flourishing phases of which we possess almost no historical vestiges. The populations which founded the cities of the Indus Valley (Mohenjo-Daro and Harappa in present day Pakistan) about 2400 B.C., cities contemporaneous with Sumer and Ur in Mesopotamia, are supplanted by the invading Aryan hordes. These Aryan invaders are a pastoral people of Indo-European extraction who migrate along with their flocks and horses from regions situated between the northern shore of the Black Sea and the Caspian Sea. About 1500 B.C., they destroy the ancient Indus Valley civilization and progressively push the prehistoric population (a dark-skinned race related to the

Large standing Buddha carved at Mathura in the fourth century. This work executed in red sandstone, with its flat draperies and wide halo, is one of the most celebrated creations of the Gupta period. The Buddha is shown attaining perfect Knowledge. (Museum of Mathura)

White marble Buddha from Amaravati (fourth century A.D.). The Buddha image progressively arises with its distinctive features : the head is crowned with a coil of hair symbolizing the cranial protuberance, or ushnisha, mark of predestination; the lobes of the ears have been stretched by the heavy jewels Gautama wore in his youth as Prince Siddharta; the eyes are half-closed so as to suggest inner meditation. (Museum of Delhi)

In Gandharan art, the moustaches of Scythian warriors adorn the lip of the ruler crowned with a diadem complete with cockade. (Museum of Delhi)

modern Dravidians) towards the south. A series of Aryan invasions which take place about the same time as those of the Achaeans and, somewhat later on, the Dorians in the eastern Mediterranean, submerge the country. Aryan ascendancy is grounded chiefly on the mastery of iron. These nomadic horsemen possess an essentially pastoral civilization. They bring with them their beliefs and ceremonies, as well as an oral tradition of sacred chants and invocations which will give birth, in the first millenium B.C., to the great Vedic texts and the Brahmanic religion, the ancestor of Hinduism properly speaking.

The Vedic religion is based on the texts of the Atharva Veda and Rig Veda, collections of hymns completed about 800 B.C., by the philosophical treatises known as the Upanishads. The absolute Being is Brahma, the uncreated and eternal spirit. Brahma may be considered as Brahma the Creator and created one, Vishnu the Protector and Shiva the Destroyer. All the other deities of the Hindu pantheon are fundamentally associated with or derived from this basic trinity. The created Brahma lives during a given divine cycle and is then succeeded by another Brahma in accordance with the supreme Law. The cycle birth-death-rebirth which binds the universe inspires the theory of reincarnation, based on the notion of retribution and rewards for individual merits.

The Birth of Buddhism and the Art of Sanchi

The historical Buddha Sakyamuni lived between 565 and 486 B.C. At the age of forty, the Enlightened One sets forth the Dharma, i.e. the Norm. This new doctrine preached by Gautama Buddha is likened to the "Turning of the Wheel of the Law". Sublime wisdom consists essentially in the abolition of suffering by way of purity, compassion and austerity. This reform embraces a series of notions peculiar to the Hindu world. Nevertheless it is soon proclaimed unorthodox. In spite of this official condemnation, the new faith gains ground and asserts its authority, especially when King Asoka (third century B.C.) becomes a devout Bud-

dhist and establishes the new religion throughout his empire, never disavowing a tolerant and pacifist moral philosophy.

Sanchi, in central India, is the birthplace of the first great stone monuments of the Buddhist religion, inspired by the cult of the historical Buddha. Three hundred years after the death of Gautama Buddha, about 220 B.C., the Maurya dynasty erects at Sanchi enormous gravemounds : the stupas. These massive brick dome-like constructions encased in sandstone are built to commemorate the tomb of the Great Teacher.

The stupa is crowned with a mast supporting three superposed stone disks meant to represent the umbrellas, or chattas, emblems of dignity, in the shade of which the Buddha meditated. The stupa itself is flanked by high gates, or toranas, opening in four directions. The sacred area is enclosed within a stone fence made up of two tiers of colossal railings joined by flights of stairs. These lofty barriers are modelled after the wooden constructions primitively erected around places of worship ; tenons and mortises are faithfully copied in stone. The balustrade marks the bounds of the consecrated area. The Buddhist rite of circumambulation was performed within the limits of this enclosure.

The gates characterized by superposed lintels are also developed from primitive wooden prototypes. Indeed, all the technical details of the

Two works from the Kushan period representing yakshis, or tree-nymphs, carved in red sandstone (second to fourth centuries A.D.). The ideal of female beauty here portrayed ressembles that already seen at Sanchi : full breasts, wide hips, wasp waist. These graceful figures are part of the decoration of the railings surrounding Buddhist stupas. Their naked bodies are adorned with jewellery and supple draperies. (Museum of Mathura)

ornamentation draw their inspiration from the same source. On the toranas at Sanchi, we see a flowering of admirable sculptural carvings. The subjects portrayed furnish us with information about the symbols of the Buddhist religion and day-to-day life.

In addition to the superb tree-nymph, symbol of the fecund energy of nature, which decorates a post of the southern gate, we should mention the low reliefs adorning the lintels. These carvings represent the life and legends of the Buddha. The Buddha himself, however, is never represented. Indeed, sculptors have not yet dared depict the image of "him whose essence is perfect knowledge". The stupa, symbolizing his death, or Nirvana, the wheel of his preaching, or chakra, his footprints, or padukas, and the bodhi tree, representing his Enlightenment, were sufficient to indicate the symbolical presence of the Buddha.

But the low reliefs at Sanchi also provide us with a panorama of the sumptuous life of Buddhist India with its glittering processions led by elephants, the wild luxuriance of ambient nature, the fortified towns surrounded by high defensive walls crowned with wooden galleries, and even the flocks and herds, wealth of the pasture-lands...

Symbol of meditation and serenity, this red sandstone Buddha, a creation of Mathura carvers (fifth century A.D.), is remarkable for its full forms and extremely delicate and austere features. (Museum of Mathura)

View of the cliff housing the Buddhist cave temples at Ajanta. This steep gorge into which the first Buddhist hermits retired in the second century B.C. was occupied through the seventh century A.D.

Right:
Façade of a Buddhist sanctuary (Cave XIX) at Ajanta, dating from the sixth century A.D. The artificial cave entirely carved out of rock copies the forms in use in primitive wooden architecture. The entrance, preceded by a pillared porch, is topped with a wide horseshoe-shaped bay.

18

The Buddha Image and the Caves at Ajanta

The Buddha was first depicted in human form by artists in the far northern region of India, on the confines of Afghanistan and Iran. After the conquest of Alexander the Great who defeats Darius III and leads his troops all the way to the Indus (325 B.C.), a series of Indo-Greek kingdoms spring up in Bactria, Kashmir and the Gandhara province of northwestern India. The artists of these regions are influenced by western artistic traditions endowing the human figure with its full power of expression.

Through the agency of this Hellenistic trend, the canons of Greek art make their way to the borders of India proper. They give rise to an art of statuary in which the Indian deities are embellished with features formerly granted Greek gods. In the first centuries of the Christian era, the image of Apollo, combined with that of the Achaemenid warriors of Persepolis, makes its appearance in the high valleys connecting the Oxus basin with the sources of the Ganges. And we now see the style of the classic "Kouroi" of Delphi and Athens applied to a suddenly humanized Asian statuary.

Gandharan art adopts both the Greek profile and Hellentistic draperies. At times even the moustache of the Scythians (who invade the small Greco-Bactrian kingdoms about 80 B.C.) adorns the faces of the Bodhisattvas in a strange synthesis uniting Asia and Europe. Five hundred years after the death of the Enlightened One, the sculptors of the great Buddhist monasteries at Taxila in the Gandhara province make so bold as to represent Gautama himself. They henceforth know how to portray, in stucco or gray schist, the idealized nobility of the Great Teacher...

However another school of sculpture has developed at the same time, at Mathura, much farther south, on the bank of the Jumna. The

Mathura artists are destined to give the finishing touches to the Buddha image with the typical inward gaze reflecting meditation, compassion and liberation. The Kushan and Gupta dynasties (first to fifth centuries A.D.) witness the creation of dense, compact, extremely interiorized works executed in red sandstone. A mystical ardour emanates from the smooth and full, pure and austere features of the Buddha as well as from his half-closed eyes, so placid, serene and suggestive of his renouncement of the world and its temptations.

Mathura sculpture comes to a standstill on holy grounds, in the eternity of Nirvana. It lies outside the scope of earthly life. The gestures of Sakyamuni alone suggest the spiritual phases that go to make up the Great Teacher's life. A complex symbolism rich in allusions is elaborated — it shall henceforth become the basic vocabulary of Buddhist sculpture. The last echoes of western classicism, interpreted by the spirit of India, thus inspire a great art destined to give birth to a far-distant posterity in Central Asia as well as in China under the Wei and Tang dynasties, at Borobudur, Angkor, capital of the Khmer Kingdom, and even in Japan...

Mathura statuary proclaims the truth of the Buddhist message, but also its deep-seated tolerance :

"My doctrine is like the ocean :
Both, the ocean and my doctrine,
Grow deeper and deeper.
My doctrine is like water
Which washes away all stains.
My doctrine is like fire
And flame which purifies all things.
My doctrine is like the heavens,
Roomy enough to house all men,
Rich and poor, mighty and humble.
And men of all castes become brothers,
Since all are sons of the Buddha."

These two small figures perhaps represent a pair of generous donors, thanks to whom one of the caves at Ajanta was decorated.

Above left:
Low reliefs flanking the entrance of Cave XIX at Ajanta depict the dramatis personae of Buddhist iconography. The central figure is a seated Buddha making the gesture inaugurating the Turning of the Wheel of the Law.

Left:
Façade of Cave XXVI at Ajanta: we find here once again the horseshoe-shaped apertures characteristic of both Buddhist and Hindu sanctuaries. Though the inscriptions attest that the cave temples was founded in the third century, it was probably not completed before the seventh century A.D.

In the apse at the far end of the monasteries carved out of rock at Ajanta, enormous praying Buddhas preside over the assemblies of the faithful in the structure's underground "courtyard".

Facing page:
Interior of Cave XXVI, with its semicircular vault and apse housing the stupa, symbol of the cosmic egg. This monument entirely hollowed out of the cliff displays stone copies of primitive wooden arches. The columns supporting the vault separate the central nave from the two narrow side aisles. A profuse sculptural decoration covers the interior of the structure. We remark in particular a seated Buddha in the centre.

Friezes displaying a very opulent iconography crown the monolithic columns of Cave XXVI. Small Bodhisattvas flank the Buddha here preaching.

A Buddhist Thebaid : Ajanta

Carved out of the barren eminences of the Deccan plateau by the Vaghora river, the gorge into the depths of which Buddhist monks retired at the dawn of the Christian era is so isolated from the rest of the world that it was brought out of oblivion only in 1817. Religious communities devoted to meditation took up residence on the steep slopes of this small valley. In this canyon cut out of living rock by the torrential monsoon rains, the followers of the Buddha excavated a whole series of cave temples. This tremendous undertaking, ensuing from earlier isolated hermitages, is begun about the second century B.C. However the most important works date from fifth and sixth centuries A.D.

In order to satisfy the various needs of the monastic communities, two types of edifices were carved out of the hillside: on one hand, the monasteries, known as viharas, and on the other hand the temples, or chaitya halls. The viharas hollowed out of soft rock at Ajanta ressemble edifices built around a square courtyard, three sides of which house the

monks' cells. They seem to be "petrifactions" of primitive wooden monasteries. In the temples, however, primitive building techniques are even more meticulously copied in stone. Indeed, these cave temples show a whole series of features proper to carpentry, here executed in stone on the façades and in the interior of the chaitya halls. They call to mind structures now destroyed, the representation of which subsists, however, in the low reliefs at Sanchi. The chaitya halls retain for example the system of keel-shaped vaults that seems to have been currently used in wooden Buddhist constructions. The horseshoe arches we see on the façades will remain one of the main characteristics of Indian religious architecture. The inner area comprises two side aisles and a central nave.

Two rows of supports, massive polygonal columns with composite capitals, also evoke the art of carpentry. At the far end of the nave we find a stupa, the hemispherical part of which symbolizes the cosmic egg. The rite of circumambulation was performed round this essential element of the Buddhist cult. For this reason, the builders contrived a semicircular vaulted apse at the temple's far end.

This "blueprint" architecture is decorated, on the entrance façades and portals as well as in the interior, with a profusion of carvings portraying the Buddha meditating or preaching the Word of Truth. Wherever we look, the face of the Great Teacher haunts the rock. Wherever we look, effigies of the Merciful One stand out in relief amidst a lavish ornamentation.

The admirable art of Buddhist painting opens out before our eyes on the inner walls of the monasteries, or viharas. Several of these monasteries with their cells opening on to columnar arcades, display walls entirely covered with frescoes. Indian artists gave free rein here to one of mankind's richest pictorial expressions. The grace and beauty of the female body, the elegance of the Bodhisattvas are displayed in vast and intricate compositions. The country's tropical vegetation furnished the artists with daily examples of the tendency towards luxuriance so brilliantly reflected in these wall paintings.

Wall painting in Cave I at Ajanta. This work dating from the sixth century (late Gupta period) is a marvellous echo of life and sensual love.

View from the great hypostyle halls of the Buddhist monasteries (viharas) at Ellora. A wide fertile plain stretches out as far as the eye can see at the foot of the cliff housing the monuments.

The gallery of Buddhas carved in the inmost recesses of one of the monasteries at Ellora is suggestive of contemplation. Plunged in twilight, the Seven Last Buddhas seated on the traditional lotus flower watch over the monks' meditation (sixth century).

Right:
This vast monastery at Ellora (Cave XI) includes two storeys and probably dates back to the end of the eighth century. One should take note of the square pillars with their sharp outline standing out against the rock face of the cliff.

The Triumph of Tolerance : Ellora

The cliff of Ellora, an enormous mass of rock blocking the plain, rises up about a hundred kilometres (62 miles) south-west of Ajanta. From the seventh through the tenth century, this stone barrier attracted representatives of India's three great religions: Buddhists, Hindus and Jains. These diverse forms of worship coexisted here side by side as a rare example of tolerance, until a wave of persecution swept down upon the disciples of Gautama who finally succumbed.

Perfecting the models furnished by the viharas at Ajanta, the Buddhist monks at Ellora elaborated vast monasteries made up of superposed tiers carved out of rock and disposed, in some places, around an open courtyard. Hypostyle halls composed of massive square supports were hollowed out of the hillside. Wide bays open on to the fertile plain which stretches out as far as the eye can see. A fascinating dialogue is thus established between the rough rock face of the cliff and the rows of massive pillars rigorously aligned in an almost "modern" style.

In the inmost recesses of these retreats, the last Buddhist monks of India — the religion of the Merciful One, faced with the rising tide of the Hindu revival, will soon begin to wane and finally seek refuge in the high valleys of the Himalayas or emigrate and propagate its teachings throughout the countries of eastern Asia — devote their lives to meditation. Countless haloed Buddhas symbolizing the great cosmic cycles watch over the monks and assist them in their ascetic tasks:

"Blessed the solitude of the man
Who knows Truth!
Blessed he who does evil

Rock-cut hypostyle hall at Ellora. The massive square pillars form bays connected by thresholds. The light of the setting sun reaches the far end of the hall. This work of architecture dating from the eighth century is one of the last Buddhist cave temples in India.

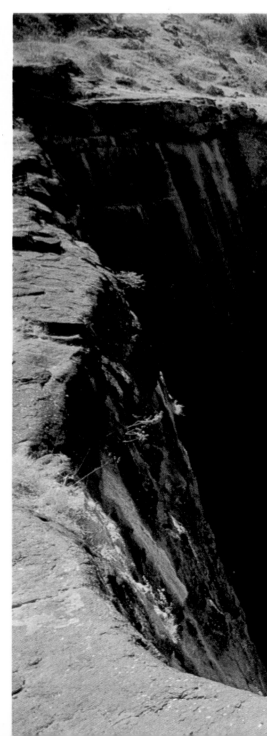

The great Shiva temple at Ellora, dating from end of the eighth century, is one of the most extraordinary achievements of Hindu architecture in India. This immense complex over 100 m (330 feet) long, entirely carved out of the cliff, entailed the removal of some 400,000 tons of rock. It ressembles a monumental open-air sculpture.

To no living creature,
And lives in compliance with the Law !
Blessed he for whom all passion,
All desire have come to an end !
Vanquish one's self,
Such is the supreme bliss !"

These galleries of meditating Buddhas, dimly lit by the glow of the setting sun, plunged in a mystical semiobscurity, may be seen as the swan song of Indian Buddhism. But the Buddha has bequeathed to Indian art a rich tradition and a set of forms which provide the basis for the aesthetics of coming centuries.

The Monumental Kailasa Temple

A profound reversal of feeling begins to appear in the fifth century and asserts itself in the seventh and eighth centuries A.D. : the ancient Vedic religion of the brahmans experiences a revival and progressively supplants Buddhism. This rebirth of the primitive rites which has its starting point among the Tamils in southern India is accompanied with a turn of the tide in favour of India's great deities : Shiva, Brahma and Vishnu. Other cults, such as those of Krishna and Kali, will soon come join these three gods par excellence.

The vigour of this Hindu revival which spreads through the central regions of the Deccan is clearly evident if we take a look at the great sanctuary entirely carved out of the cliff at Ellora in honour of Shiva and his consort Parvati. Executed during the reign of King Krishna I, from 760 to 780, the Kailasa temple is the largest monolithic edifice in India. This monumental sculpture hollowed and carved out of living rock is an immense structure 100 m (330 feet) from front to back and 75 m (250 feet) from side to side. The central tower rises up 30 m (100 feet) above the surrounding courtyard. The edifice owes its name to this tower which symbolizes the World Mountain regarded in the Hindu religion as the gods' paradise. The Kailasa — or Mount Meru — constantly reappears in the symbolism bound up with Hindu architecture.

At Ellora, the symbol reaches grandiose proportions. This colossal open-air sculpture is a fantastic stroke of skill. Unlike earlier cave temples entirely hollowed out of the hillside, the Kailasanath temple entailed the removal of the exterior rock surmounting the complex. Thus the various structures, from the gopura (or entrance gate) situated on the façade to the secondary sanctuaries crowded together at the far end of the courtyard, literally spring out of the cliff. In order to free the enormous stone pyramid composing the monolithic tower, no less than 400,000 tons of rock had to be cut away. In addition, the Kailasa temple includes underground chambers on either side of the sanctuary proper, a vast gallery with porticoes running along three sides of the edifice and an entire city of subordinate structures, with a bridge joining the gopura to the chapel dedicated to the sacred bull Nandi, to say nothing of the stone needles, 17 m (56 feet) high, held in reserve and, in the centre, an enormous hypostyle hall with 16 square pillars preceding the tower.

In addition to this titanic technical feat, the Kailasanath temple is remarkable for its rich ornamentation. Several hundred metre long low

The lofty tower of the Kailasanath temple, viewed from the summit of the cliff, symbolizes the city of the gods. It is preceded by a vast square hall, or mandapa, on the roof of which four lions keep watch. On the far right, one may distinguish the Nandi mandapa and the entrance gopura. This colossal creation is derived from sanctuaries in southern India.

This rock-cut façade indicates the size of the mandapa of the Kailasanath temple at Ellora. The man standing on the threshold gives us an idea of the scale on which this giant sanctuary was constructed. It is the largest rock-cut temple in India. The façades were originally covered with frescoes.

Right:
A stone needle, 17 m (56 feet) high, towers up on either side of the Nandi mandapa, shrine dedicated to the sacred bull associated with the god Shiva. On the far right, low reliefs illustrate scenes from the Ramayana.

reliefs depict the great scenes of the Mahabharata and the Ramayana, carved out of rock. And we should not forget that most of the chambers and façades were originally covered with frescoes. This fact explains the name given the edifice by the native population: the "Ranga Mahal", or palace of colour.

This grandiose work of art, hemmed in on three sides by tremendous vertical walls carved out of rock, cannot be viewed in proper perspective. This graceful architecture, seemingly welded to the rock face of the cliff, crushes us beneath its mass. We have the same impression of confinement as in earlier cave temples. The visitor who performs the rite of circumambulation on the bottom of the artificial "gorge" contrived between the mountain and the sanctuary, is struck with a feeling of claustrophobia when the sky disappears above him, leaving but a narrow crevice through which the sun throws a meagre light. And even if the sole reason for this impression of suffocation is a result of the architectural technique chosen which did not permit to open out wider spaces around the edifice, it nonetheless symbolizes the bond which brings earth and heaven into close relationship in Indian mysticism.

The Rise of Jainsim

Vardhamana, known among his disciples as Mahavira, the Victorious One, lived in the sixth century B.C. and was a slightly older contemporary of Buddha. Born about 540 B.C., he was destined to become one of the principal adversaries of Sakyamuni who, like himself, was of princely extraction. He led the life of a wandering ascetic, gave up clothing and opted for absolute nudism. After having attained perfect

Below:
The opulent sculptural decoration lining the galleries of the Kailasa temple depicts the various avatars of the god Shiva.

At the foot of the high cliff surrounding the Kailasanath temple at Ellora we find ring corridors and secondary shrines hollowed out of rock.

Tolerance is the directing principle at El-lora where the cliff houses rock-cut temples belonging to India's three great religions: Buddhism, Shivaism and Jainism. Here, pairs of dvarapalas (temple guardians) watch over the cella in a Hindu cave.

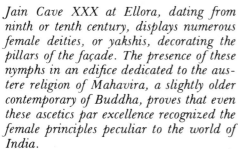

Jain Cave XXX at Ellora, dating from ninth or tenth century, displays numerous female deities, or yakshis, decorating the pillars of the façade. The presence of these nymphs in an edifice dedicated to the austere religion of Mahavira, a slightly older contemporary of Buddha, proves that even these ascetics par excellence recognized the female principles peculiar to the world of India.

Facing page:
The grace of the yakshis with their naked bodies adorned with jewels might well surprise us in Jain caves at Ellora. The Victorious One (Jina), however, by no means rejected these traditional elements of Indian iconography.

Knowledge and Nirvana, he became a Conqueror (Jina). From that time forth, his preaching achieved some success in the plain of the Ganges. When he died, however, about 468 B.C., his sect proved unable to overshadow the followers of the Buddha. Jainism begins to flourish under the Maurya dynasty, when King Chandra Gupta (fourth century A.D.) abdicates the throne and becomes an earnest adherent of the new religion.

From 800 to 1000, the Jain movement brings its contribution to the monumental creations adorning the cliffs at Ellora. And Jain cave temples enrich Indian sculpture with first-rate works of art. This is particularly true of the Little Kailasanath temple, seemingly a reduced copy of the Hindu sanctuary. We find here once again the traditional elements of Indian iconography and in particular the marvellous nymphs, carved in a very unrestrained and voluptuous style recalling the sculptural carvings at Sanchi.

Indeed, the idealization of buxom female beauty — big breasts and wide hips separated by an extremely slender wasp waist — and the vivid sensuality thus suggested are a constant and common feature of Buddhism, Hinduism and Jainism. This obsession preoccupies even the most ascetic cults. It will finally result in the exacerbations of tantric "erotism" and the analogous Buddhist doctrine, the Vehicle of Lightning. The Bodhisattvas are furnished with wives, the Taras, and the activity of the divinity is symbolized by the union of the sexes. Desire is believed to be abolished by its realization.

The Shore Temple at Mamallapuram in southern India is one of the first sanctuaries built in the Dravidian style characteristic of the Hindu resurgence. Erected in the eighth century on a promontory on the Coromandel Coast, it has withstood the ocean's wrath for over twelve hundred years.

Right:
Work of the Pallava dynasty, the Shore Temple at Mamallapuram is built entirely in granite. It displays a series of rising tiers of decreasing dimensions representing the abode of the gods on Mount Meru —— equivalent to Mount Kailasa.

34

The Influence of Southern India

The revival experienced by the ancient Vedic religion has its starting point in the southern regions of India where time-honoured Dravidian rites are combined with Brahmanic cults to give birth to what is now known as Hinduism. The first Hindu sanctuaries are built under the Chalukya dynasty. The sites of Aihole and Badami are the cradle of this sacred architecture which will progressively conquer the whole of India and a large part of Southeast Asia, from Burma to Java via Indo-China and the kingdom of Angkor.

When the Pallava dynasty triumphs over the Chalukyas, monarchs draw inspiration from the temples at Aihole and undertake to reproduce them carved out of rock. In the seventh century, King Narasimhavaram I decides to found a trading port on the east coast (Bay of Bengal). Near the beach shaded by palm trees, a site strewn with enormous granite boulders catches the ruler's attention. The new capital will be built here, at Mamallapuram. The sanctuaries will be carved out of these colossal boulders. The ships built for the spice trade will leave this port and propagate the traditions of Indian art throughout the Indian Archipelago and the Khmer kingdom (modern Cambodia).

The Rock Temples at Mamallapuram

The complex at Mamallapuram is made up of a whole series of temples, a vast low relief depicting the Descent of the Ganges, a group of Seven

Below left:
Near Mamallapuram, the Tiger Cave houses a small shrine the lintel of which is supported by two raging lions. The mouth of the artificial cave is surrounded by tiger's heads carved out of granite.

Detail of the low relief depicting the Descent of the Ganges at Mamallapuram.

Pagodas representing petrified processional chariots, and finally the famous Shore Temple, built on a rocky promontory. Its high tower calls to mind a lighthouse occupying an advanced post on the magnificent Coromandel Coast.

The oldest group, dating from about 650 A.D., is that of the Seven Pagodas or Raths (processional chariots). These structures carved out of granite reflect ancient types of wooden vehicles. They furnish us with information on the architecture of small mobile shrines and the details of their construction, copied after the techniques of carpentry — as also in the Buddhist caves at Ajanta. This complex which remained unfinished, had an eminently symbolic aspect: the inner spaces, hollowed out of a monolithic granite mass, are extremely confined. The cella has just enough room to admit an officiant, for the sacrificial rites.

The most interesting feature of this architecture still in embryo, is the ornamentation of the roofs. The roofs of the Mamallapuram temples are generally made up of a series of steps rising up to heaven. Their form is not unlike the pyramids of Egypt. The ascending tiers are decorated with little pavilions. We may also notice rounded roofs — modelled on primitive thatch roofing — and horseshoe-shaped pediments — similar to those adorning the façades of the chaitya halls at Ajanta. The tower built in the shape of a step-pyramid (like the Kailasanath temple at Ellora) is a replica of Mount Meru, the World Mountain. We thus find here once again the symbolic representation of the heavenly city, paradise inhabited by the gods.

In addition, the plan which accounts for the finished form of the

Among the petrified processional chariots at Mamallapuram we see the Nakulasahadeo with, on the right, the elephant supposed to draw it.

Right:
The entrance to the Rath of Draupadi is guarded by two gracious deities.

Overleaf (36-37):
The group of the Seven Pagodas, or Raths (processional chariots), carved out of granite boulders at Mamallapuram in the seventh century A.D. under the Pallava dynasty. From right to left: the Rath of Draupadi, in the shape of a hut with a palm leaf roof; the pyramidal Rath of Arjuna; the two-storeyed Rath of Bhima with a barrel-roof like the chaitya halls; and the Dharmaraja Rath with its high pyramidal roof, the prototype of the Kailasa temple at Ellora. Last of all, in the foreground, the sacred bull Nandi.

Eastern façade of the Rath of Arjuna with its sculptures dedicated to the god Indra.

Left:
The Raths carved out of granite boulders on the shore at Mamallapuram are adorned with enchanting female deities. In spite of thirteen centuries of bad weather and monsoon rains, their smiles are as captivating and mysterious as ever.

Above:
The two-storeyed Rath of Bhima with its columns standing on effigies of lions. The lower level of the roof is decorated with miniature pavilions symbolizing the dwellings of the gods.

Dharmaraja Rath at Mamallapuram, for example, is conceived wholly on the basis of a geometric figure known as a mandala. The figure in question represents a sort of magic network encompassing the edifice's structure. The aim of the mandala, esoteric diagram the origins of which date back to the pre-Christian Vedic world, is to bring the world here below into harmony with the heavens. Henceforth, temples are built in the likeness of the universe. This explains why the arrangement of the sanctuary — as also town planning in general — is regarded as a miniature replica of the abode of the gods.

The mandala is a circular figure inscribed in a square itself subdivided into a chequer-board comprising a given number of unities (padas). This number may vary from one mandala to another, according to the complexity of the diagram. These variations correspond to a precise meaning. Depending on whether the side of the square is divided into 2, 3, 4, 5 or 6 padas (etc.), the resulting chequer-board contains 4, 9, 16, 25 or 36 (etc.) squares. As we see, this series is based on a simple geometrical progression. We often hear of mandalas comprising 8, 16 or even 32 padas on each side.

This diagram legible in a plane may quite naturally be transposed into three-dimensional space by means of a vertical projection. In this case, the mandala gives rise to a pyramid composed of a series of steps of decreasing dimensions. We may well imagine all the implications Indian artists — fascinated by numerology — drew from this principle. We find the mandala in use in all regions influenced by Hindu thought, in par-

Detail of an elephant gazing on the Descent of the Ganges.

Left:
Descent of the Ganges, rock relief at Mamallapuram. This masterpiece of Pallava sculpture covers an area of 240 square metres (287 square yards) and represents the miracle by which Shiva made the Ganges come down to earth.

Right:
The Dharmaraja Rath at Mamallapuram, prototype of later Dravidian sanctuaries, includes three storeys decorated with miniature pavilions and crowned with an octagonal dome.

Bronze sculpture which flourishes under the Chola dynasty in southern India marks the apogee of medieval Indian statuary. These works dating from the tenth through the thirteenth century bear witness to a remarkable mastery of the so-called lost-wax process. Parvati, Shiva's consort, is here wearing a most seductive garment. (Museum of Dalhi)

Above right:
Shiva, bearing an emblematic axe and endowed with four arms to better attest his omnipotence, is here portrayed in the so-called pose of Dakshinamurti, "he who faces south".

Right:
The beautiful Sita, wife of Rama, in a relaxed pose. Her head-dress differs from that of Parvati but the gestures are the same. She is adorned with sumptuous ritual jewelery. Her only garment is a piece of cloth draped about her legs after the manner peculiar to southern India. This Chola bronze dates from the tenth century. (Museum of Delhi)

ticular at Borobudur in the plains of central Java where the Great Stupa, built in the eight century, is a three-dimensional rendering of the same magic diagram.

It is moreover quite possible that the unfinished Seven Pagodas at Mamallapuram were mere models. Their dwarfish cellae may never have sheltered the rites of Hinduism. It indeed seems quite probable that the ruler who erected these factitious monuments wished to celebrate the divinity by means of an eternal procession, a colossal and indestructible offering, rather than to raise a complex of veritable sanctuaries in his honour.

The Shore Temple, dating from the eighth century, is built according to the same magic and religious principles. The pyamidal roof is composed of repeated granite cornices. The high tower crowning the cella is preceded by a second, smaller tower, foretelling perhaps the duality characteristic of classical temples in which the cella proper is given a counterpart : the assembly hall (mandapa).

The Shore Temple, built on a terrace jutting into the ocean and protected by enormous granite blocks polished by the waves and ressembling monstrous elephant's backs, has braved the elements for twelve centuries. Neither the wrath of a sea in which typhoons are no rarity nor the torrential monsoon rains have shaken it. The sculptural carvings, however, executed in hard granite by the skilful artists of the Pallava dynasty, are now eroded, smoothed down and almost worn away.

Facing page:
The most famous manifestation of Shiva: the Lord of Dance, or Nataraja. This admirable Chola bronze dating from the twelfth century represents Shiva as the personification of universal energy, endowed with four arms, surrounded by a fiery crown, trampling a demon underfoot.

This Chola bronze from the thirteenth century represents Krishna, the most important manifestation of Vishnu, here portrayed as a graceful and mischievous youth. One should take note of his very smooth and polished complexion. (Museum of Delhi)

Axe-bearing god: perhaps Shiva, perhaps one of the avatars of Vishnu, the god Paraçurama, "Rama the axe-bearer". (Museum of Delhi)

Bronze Sculpture under the Chola Dynasty

In 846 the Kingdom of the Pallavas is overturned by the Chola dynasty, the members of which rule over the whole of southern India through the end of the thirteenth century. They erect, about 1000, the great temple at Tanjore. This brilliant dynasty also affirms its authority in the field of sculpture. In the tenth century, we witness the birth of an admirable art of bronze statuary, made by the lost wax process. This technique requires first of all a wax model which is encased in a plaster cast. The mould is then heated in order to melt the wax which will be replaced by melted bronze. The mould must be broken in order to recuperate the finished work which is then finely chiselled and polished.

The masterpieces of this Tamil art which reaches its peak in the eleventh and twelfth centuries, are for the most part representations of Hindu deities. Shiva and his female counterpart Parvati are doubtless the most remarkable creations of this art stressing purity and idealization. Each gesture, scrupulously indexed and classified, takes on a precise symbolic meaning. The nudity of the bodies, perfectly rendered by the polished bronze surfaces, is set off by rich jewelled ornaments and elegantly arranged draperies.

In southern India, this metal sculpture supplants stone statuary which continues to flourish in Orissa, both at Bhubaneswar and at Konarak, and in the Gangetic plain, south of the Jumna, at Khajuraho.

The oldest sanctuary at Khajuraho, anterior to 900 A.D., is the Chaunsath Yogini temple, built in granite blocks. It is dedicated to the sixty-four female ascetics who escorted Kali the Redoubtable. Sixty-four shrines originally rose up around the great goddess's cella. Only thirty-five have been preserved.

The Lakshmana temple at Khajuraho (on the right), dating from the mid-tenth century, is built on a terrace the four corners of which lodge secondary shrines. The complex is dedicated to Vishnu. On the left, the Vahara and Matangeshwara temples.

Khajuraho : a Hymn to Love

In the boundless plain of the Jumna (or Yamuna), tributary of the Ganges, the Khajuraho temples rise up among clusters of tropical trees like genuine jungle cathedrals. Their lofty, finely carved stone spires soar up to heaven in what seems a tremendous burst of fervour expressive of the sublime aspirations of the faith peculiar to medieval India. The visitor who draws near these monuments surrounded by luxuriant vegetation is surprised to discover the abundance of sculptural carvings decorating the façades and disposed in a rigorous order bound by architectonic lines of force, similar to that employed in more or less contemporaneous European masterpieces such as the tympanum of Autun or the portals of Chartres.

During the tenth to the twelfth century of the Christian era, the Chandella dynasty — which establishes its capital at Khajuraho — reaches the peak of its power. At the same time the Muslims make ever more frequent raids into northern India. The Chandella rulers successfully counter the attacks of Sultan Mahmud of Ghazni in 1091. In 1202, however, they are defeated by Mohammed of Ghor. A century will go by before they come under the rule of the sultans of Dehli, in 1310.

A Holy Place of Hindu Art

In the meantime, their formerly brilliant capital city which sheltered no less than eighty-five Hindu and Jain sanctuaries, is already in decay. Life is ebbing away and the splendid seat of power is soon merely a straggling village. The defeat inflicted by the Muslim troops marks the beginning of an irremediable downfall. Henceforth the jungle resumes possession of the site which will thus be preserved from the ravages of Muslim iconoclasm. The ancient capital, lost in rank jungle overgrowth, will be rediscovered by the English in 1840. They extract the city from its leafy gangue and restore the twenty odd subsisting temples, among the greatest architectural and sculptural monuments of the late Medieval period.

A stone skeleton is all that now remains of this city which elaborated an astonishing art. Indeed, while several sanctuaries, though left for five hundred years to the whims of nature, are extraordinarily well preserved, all the secular architecture, the dwellings and palace complexes, built in wood, thatch and mud bricks, have completely disappeared. Nonetheless, the Chandella capital was doubtless an enormous city : the monuments which have survived intact are spread over an area of over 4 km (2.5 miles). Now the lofty towers of the sanctuaries alone bear witness to the ancient splendour of this city which was one of the holy places of the Hindu faith.

Sculpture at Khajuraho representing the god Vishnu endowed with four arms and bearing his traditional emblems: club, conch, disk and lotus.

Great tower, or sikhara, of the Kandarya Mahadeo temple at Khajuraho, dating from about 1050. A cluster of small pinnacles buttresses the main spire, 31 m (102 feet) high.

Below:
Detail of a pinnacle. The entire surface is made up of tiny kudus (horseshoe-shaped apertures) symbolizing the dwellings of the gods on Mount Meru.

Medieval Sanctuaries

The forms first elaborated in the temples at Aihole and Mamallapuram in the region of southern India which may be called the cradle of Hindu architecture, continue to evolve and grow ever richer. Complementary spaces are added to the sanctuary, originally limited to one tower alone. This process of mutation takes place in Orissa, on the east coast of the Indian peninsula. Both at Bhubaneswar and at Konarak, the tower (sikhara) housing the statue of the god or the lingam (phallic symbol) associated with Shiva is preceded by an assembly hall known in different regions as the mandapa or jagamohan. The two inner spaces thus created are joined by a door. Viewed from the outside, they make up two distinct entities and may be directly preceded by yet a third separate structure, the dance pavilion.

In the course of the evolution undergone by the forms of the Hindu sanctuary, these three entities come together to make up an organic whole. This amalgamation gives rise to the classical medieval temple, as seen for example at Khajuraho. Such is the division of space employed in the admirable Kandarya Mahadeo temple (1050), the most celebrated of the Khajuraho sanctuaries. The three main divisions are here preceded by a vestibule and set off with a series of buttressing porches flanking both the mandapa and the tower so as to form a sort of double transept.

Like a never-ending burst of fervour, the roofs of the Kandarya Mahadeo temple at Khajuraho, built about 1050, soar up to heaven. The four steps culminating in the spire top the vestibule, the dance pavilion, the mandapa, or assembly hall, and last of all the cella housing the lingam (phallic symbol) and the statue of the god.

When one views the edifice in profile, one may distinguish its various components joined together in a harmonious progression accentuated by the increasing height of the roofs. A series of projections corbeled inward thus leads up to the top of the spire. An overhanging roof tops the entrance vestibule. A steep staircase leads up to this structure which is supported by four pillars and ressembles a sort of narthex. Wide bays open on to the outside. The vestibule thus serves as a transition from the profane world to the universe of the temple. The temple itself has no enclosure wall. It is built on a high pedestal, or temenos.

Inner Space

The covered entrance precedes the artha mandapa, originally a dance pavilion, here an open structure composed of a group of twelve pillars, four of which are engaged in the wall at the far end. Here too, the pillars support an overhanging corbeled roof made up of repeated stone cornices. The mandapa proper includes four massive pillars forming a central square. This assembly hall is dimly lighted by the side porches. The prevailing semiobscurity lends itself to sacred mysteries. The roof, soaring up even higher than the two preceding ones, is flanked by a multitude of small pinnacles. The cella (garbha griha) plunged in gloom houses the lingam and the statue of the god. It is surrounded by a narrow ring corridor opening on to the two arms of the second transept and a sort of apse, identical with the side porches. The temple is built in the shape of a Lorraine cross. The apse and transepts provide a solid foundation for the high-soaring lyricism of the lofty tower crowning the cel-

Facing page (above):
On the façades at the base of the tower of the Kandarya Mahadeo temple, sculptures derived from tantric doctrines extoll the mithunas, or divine lovers, who perform the sex act in various postures, both sophisticated and symbolic. Copulation is believed to represent the soul's union with the divinity.

Facing page (below):
Open porches of the Kandarya Mahadeo temple.

Below:
A troop of gracious apsaras (nymphs) frolicing round the deities, exhibit the sensuality inherent in ancient rites of fecundity. They shrink from neither seductive adornments nor suggestive poses.

The lovers carved on the façades of the Khajuraho temples, with their conventionalized features and erotic poses, give voice to mankind's yearning for divine oneness.

Lika a garland round the god Shiva, the apsaras shamelessly voice their desire and bare their voluptuous bodies.

Above right :
The carvings decorating the balustrades which surround the porches of the Kandarya Mahadeo temple seem to be chiselled in wood. One should take note of the tiny scenes carved at the base.

Above :
An apsara sways her hips and gazes on her image in a mirror.

la. An orderly profusion of pinnacles flanks this main tower with its curved outline, ressembling a stone prayer rising up to heaven. The massive masonry and sculptural decorations are indeed all-important in Hindu temple architecture.

The tower of Kandarya Mahadeo is 30 m (100 feet) high and is in itself alone expressive of deep faith. The lavish geometric ornamentation covering its sides makes frequent use of the horseshoe motif (kudu) already seen in the chaitya halls at Ajanta and the raths at Mamallapuram. However, it is here reproduced in miniature as a mere detail of the decoration. This motif evokes the dwellings of the gods on Mount Meru and the rising tiers which go to make up paradise. Thanks to its presence the tower, or sikhara, becomes an image of the divine city believed to be the axis of the world.

The most bewildering revelation of this medieval art is the profusion of lavish sculptural carvings which decorate the façades of the temples. Gods and nymphs galore frolic on these walls literally clothed in statues. Their generalized and abstracted features as well as the very sensuous

The apsaras at Khajuraho, faithful servants of Shiva, are sometimes smiling sometimes sulky. All alike are characterized by round full breasts, jewellery intended to enhance their beauty and gauzy clinging draperies. Actually they hardly seem naked, as if these ornaments were but a component part of the ritual.

Left:
Humour is not lacking in this art of sacred sculpture peculiar to medieval India: this apsara appears to feel ill at ease at the sight of a scandalous scene.

Corridor encompassing the cella of the Kandarya Mahadeo temple at Khajuraho. The apsaras continue to dance in the twilight which prevails in the sanctuary, dimly lighted by the side porches.

The cella dedicated to the god Shiva, viewed from the mandapa, or assembly hall with its massive pillars crowned with capital widening out towards the top. In the holy of holies out of the Kandarya Mahadeo temple, the marble lingam (phallus) rises up in front of the statue of the god.

gestures which bring to life their voluptuous bodies portrayed in wholly unrestrained poses, give voice to a song of universal love.

A Song of Universal Love

This cult is inspired by tantric mysticism which regards the performance of the sex act as a liberation of man's fundamental energies in obedience to cosmic laws and a means of attaining ecstasy. It is a transposition of ancient pre-Aryan rites of fecundity. In a temple dedicated to the lingam, phallic symbol and emblem of Shiva, this exaltation of carnal joys is indeed the most sublime image of love we can imagine. In Hindu India, erotic love reflects a universal desire for union, for the fusion of duality in divine oneness.

All is grace·and beauty in this poem dedicated to life. While the lascivious postures and masterly scenes of copulation may well have shocked the first Westerners who visited Khajuraho, it is no longer possible to regard these marvellous sculptures as mere "erotic", not to say pornographic images. Western taboos are unknown in Indian civilization. The sculptures at Khajuraho are well and truly a glorification of supreme bliss, alone capable of abolishing evil and doing away with suffering.

Among the swarming mass of sculptures, delicate ornamental motifs chiselled in stone recall the art of wood carving.

Above:
Extraordinary heavenward soaring of the sikhara wich crowns the Kandarya Mahadeo temple at Khajuraho like the spire of a cathedral. It is in fact the image of paradise, pivot of the world and abode of the gods on Mount Meru.

The Sanctuary of a Thousand Gods : Madura

The god Shiva mounted on the sacred bull Nandi rules over the temple at Madura, built in the seventeenth century in southern India.

Left:
The baroque and disorderly sculptural decoration of the gopuras (monumental gates) of the temple at Madura associates traditional Hindu deities with the demons of the ancient Tamil cults.

Facing page:
The incredible gopuras at Madura: a swarming mass of gods, goddesses and Mythical monsters symbolizes the divine city. The polychrome ornamentation is the result of recent restoration.

Before dealing with the Muslim period beginning at the end of the thirteenth century with the conquest of northern India by Islam, we should first like to stress the importance of the last monuments erected by Hindu rulers in the southern part of the peninsula which remained independent. Indeed, for a brief period even the far south fell into the hands of the Muslim conquerors who founded a sultanate at Madura in the sixteenth century. However, the Tamils soon got the upper hand and threw out the invaders. Hinduism then experienced an extremely vigorous resurgence and inspired an entirely regenerated art characterized by a luxuriance well in keeping with ambient tropical nature.

A City of Temples

The Great Temple at Madura is built under the Nayak dynasty which rules from the sixteenth to the eighteenth century. The sanctuary, dedicated to a revelation of Shiva and his female counterpart Parvati, was erected between 1623 and 1660. It is a colossal complex of halls and galleries enclosed within a wall almost a kilometre round. High towers,

The sacred pool at Madura surrounded by wide stairways and a roofed gallery. Thousands of worshippers come to bathe here on Hindu holidays.

Facing page:
Ganesha, the elephant-headed god, son of Shiva and his gracious consort Parvati, sculptured in stucco at Madura. We find here once again the peculiar garment draped about the legs worn by bronze goddesses under the Chola dynasty.

or gopuras, mark the entrances to the sacred enclosure. The outer enclosure wall contains two others, concentrically disposed, as well as a fourth inner enclosure surrounding a secondary shrine and yet a fifth one encompassing a sacred pool almost 50 m (165 feet) long. Each of these enclosure walls is equipped with its own gopuras. The towers decrease in height as they come closer to the central place of worship. The gopura marking the south entrance is over 55 m (180 feet) high and includes no less than ten stories. On the other hand, the convex curves characteristic of medieval sikharas, corbeled inward, are here inverted so as to form concave lines; the heavenward movement thus acquires an extreme elegance.

This new formula, incorporating the highest architectural elements at the periphery, revolutionizes the traditions of classical sanctuaries, the height of which increased towards the centre and culminated in the sikhara crowning the cella. Thus the holy of holies, formerly the most conspicuous element of the temple, is constantly whittled down in the late architecture of southern India. In return, the great gates opening in four directions reach truly gigantic proportions and are covered with a profuse sculptural ornamentation.

The series of gopuras — the temple enclosure includes eleven — tower

above a jumbled complex of chambers and courtyards calling to mind an enormous labyrinth. In this chaos, the swarming mass of worshippers walking in procession under the porticoes or making their way towards the waters of the sacred pool, reflects the swarming mass of rigidly gesticulating, mannered deities haunting the façades of the polychrome towers. Thousands of statues painted with vivid colours occupy each story of the gopuras. This polychrome ornamentation is the result of a daring restoration undertaken thirty years ago with a view to re-creating the original appearance of the temple complex.

The gopuras have now taken the place of the sikharas. Rising up at the four cardinal points, they symbolize the divine city crowning Mount Meru, the sacred and paradisiac dwelling-place of the gods. In order to understand the energy and vitality characteristic of this late art, one must contemplate this lavish entanglement of sculptural decorations portraying gods, monsters and nymphs. This rococo profusion of elaborate sculptures, this polychrome ornamentation comparable to the contemporaneous creations of Hispano-Mexican baroque, bear witness to the vigour of Hinduism among the Dravidian populations of southern India. For we must not forget that while Madura is assuredly the most spectacular of these late temple complexes, numerous similar pro-

These representations of the sacred bull Nandi, crowning the ridge of the roofs of the temple at Madura, flank a minor deity.

Left:
One of Shiva's southern avatars: the wrathful god dancing the tandava mimes the destruction of the universe and the end of a cosmic cycle. With his flaming sword he lays low a demon representing the old world, now accursed. He has eight pairs of arms and bears a series of emblems of divinity. His terrifying face is an embodiment of anger: this is Shiva the Destroyer.

ductions may be found at Sriringam, Kancheepuram and elsewhere.

Unlike this wholly indigenous art, the Hindu creations of northern India betray at times the influence of Muslim architecture.

The Muslim presence in the plain of the Ganges gives rise to a mixed style, in which the mutual "contaminations" are often of great interest. Thus the Golden Temple of Shiva, or Vishwanath, erected in 1777 at Benares displays a gold-plated bulb-shaped dome inspired by Mogul creations.

We can now observe a marked difference between the far south, impervious to Muslim contributions, and the north, where centuries of foreign occupation finally get the better of local styles and customs.

The bulb-shaped gold-plated dome of the Golden Temple of Shiva, or Vishwanath, at Benares. This sanctuary erected in the great holy city of eastern India betrays the influence of Mogul architecture.

The Conquest of India by Islam

A short time after the Hegira, the Muslims launch a naval expedition in the Arabian sea and plunder the coasts of India (637). In 712, land forces led by Mohammed ibn Qasim invade the Sind province and reach Multan, in the very heart of the Indus Valley, where Muslim troops encounter war elephants for the first time. They nevertheless gain the victory.

Beginning in 986, it is the turn of the Ghaznevid dynasty, rulers of a Turkish tribe settled in the mountainous region surrounding Ghazni, to make raids into the Indian plains. Peshawar surrenders and the Khyber pass which commands access to the plain of the Ganges falls into the hands of the Muslim invaders. Between 1000 and 1026, Mahmud of Ghazni, the first Muslim ruler to bear the title of sultan, sends out no less than seventeen expeditions which put to sack the towns of northern India. He takes Mathura in 1018. After each raid, however, he returns to his eagle's nest, laden with riches and dragging thousands of Indian slaves in his wake. Mahmud does not seek to occupy the country. He is quite content with plundering the rich Hindu cities.

The Muslims at Dehli

Mahmud of Ghazni's successors are less warlike. A usurper, Mohammed of Ghor, the ablest of the Shansabani sultans, dethrones them and assumes power. He takes Ghazni in 1151, adopts Mahmud's policy of spoliation and is not long in putting it into practice. He swoops down upon Khanua and Benares. A large part of northern India comes under his rule. Before returning to his mountain hide-out, he appoints his general Qutb ud-Din Aibak governor of Delhi. When Mohammed dies, Qutb ud-Din is chosen king by the army. He is the first independent Muslim emperor of India. He assumes the title of Sultan of Delhi and founds the Slave dynasty which rules from 1206 to 1290.

As a mark of Muslim ascendancy in India, Qutb ud-Din has decided to erect at Delhi a mosque crowned with a tremendous minaret intended as a tower of victory. The construction of the Qutb Minar is begun in 1199. This star-shaped turret, 72.5 m (238 feet) high, displays sharp edges alternating with rounded ribs. The upper stories, corbeled inward, put rhythm into the heavenward motion of the conical structure. Similar towers are not uncommon in Persian architecture. Indeed, the artistic vocabulary destined to serve as a basis for the architecture of Muslim India has its birthplace in the Iranian world. It receives however the imprint of Hindu techniques, in particular as regards the use of stone which henceforth replaces the characteristic brickwork of Persian constructions.

As for the mosque itself, known as Quwwat al-Islam (might of Islam),

Detail of the first corbeled balcony of the Qutb Minar at Delhi. In order to stress the minaret's religious significance, an epigraphic frieze of Koranic texts runs round the tower. The stalactite-like structures are derived from contemporaneous Persian art.

Left:
The Qutb Minar, 72.5 m (238 feet) high, erected in 1199 by Qutb ud-Din Aibak, the first independent sultan to rule over the plain of the Ganges, was intended as a mark of Muslim ascendancy in India.

63

The Alai Derwaze gate raised in 1305 in front of the Quwwat al-Islam ("might of Islam") mosque at Delhi. This monument with its red sandstone façades inlaid with white marble heralds the typical creations of the Mogul period.

All the hypostyle halls of the great Quwwat al-Islam mosque are composed of pillars recuperated from Hindu temples destroyed by the order of the sultants of Delhi.

the ruler simply reuses elements of Hindu temples destroyed by his order.

When Qutb ud-Din dies, Sultan Iltutmish comes to the throne and rules over Delhi from 1211 to 1235. He pushes back the advance guard of the Mongolians who attempt to force their way into India through the mountain passes on the north. We should not forget that under Genghis-Khan the warlike Mongolian hordes are in power not only in Samarkand and Khorezm but also in Peking and the whole of China... Iltutmish is buried in a tomb erected behind the Quwwat al-Islam mosque. His cube-shaped mausoleum, built in Indo-Persian style, is crowned with a typically Persian dome. The gate built by Ala ud-Din Khalji in 1311 and christened Alai Derwaze displays alternating patterns in red sandstone and white marble. This technique remains one of the principal characteristics of Muslim architecture in northern India.

In the meantime, the Mongolian danger is becoming more and more pressing. In 1245 the invaders are thrown back once again. Fifty years later they reappear, plunder Lahore and advance against Delhi. However they do not succeed in capturing the Muslim capital. The Tughluq dynasty, then ruling at Delhi, pushes the invading hordes back yet a third time. Mohammed ibn Tughluq (1325-1351) resolves to transfer his capital from Delhi to Daulatabad, formerly known as Deogir, near Ellora. He hopes thus to elude the Mongolian threat and get a firmer grip on his possessions in the Deccan. He builds a new city around the ruins of a tremendous Hindu fortress and makes no scruple to deport the entire population of Delhi to this new capital, 1000 km (620 miles) farther south.

Over ten thousand people fall victim to the rigours of this forced journey and never reach their destination.

Those who arrive safely discover for their habitation a veritable Muslim Carcassonne rising up in the middle of a wide and fertile plain. The city, surrounded by three concentric enclosure walls bristling with barbicans, is spread out around the enormous mass of rock composing

The massive walls of the second enceinte at Daulatabad. This fortified town, built in the first half of the fourteenth century by Mohammed ibn Tughluq in the region of Ellora, was meant to replace Delhi as the capital of the sultanate. However the new city remained the centre of the Muslim empire for only three short years. Its ruins may still be seen in the plain. They bear witness to one of Muslim India's most extravagant undertakings.

Left:
Palaces and tombs still lie strewn about the plain at Danlatabad, recalling an ephemeral period of glory followed by a brief reoccupation terminating in the fifteenth century.

65

the fortress, whose naturally steep cliffs have been recut to a perfect perpendicular, rendering it stormproof.

Yet it is not long before Mohammed ibn Tughluq realizes that the site does not meet with his requirements and decides to abandon Daulatabad and return to Dehli. Only a few short years after their first odyssey, the city's inhabitants are obliged to forsake this stronghold with its gigantic walls, posterns and outworks, about-turn and undergo the hardships of the return trip.

Shortly afterwards India is seething with discontent. Mohammed ibn Tughluq loses his grip on the empire. The Hindu revival gains ground in the south and the Tamils cast off the Muslim yoke. A division of power in the north accompanies these rebellions.

The Mongolians Victorious

In 1397, Tamerlane, at the head of ninety thousand Mongolian horsemen, takes the cities of Multan and Delhi. He ruthlessly slaughters the inhabitants of northern India. The countryside bathes in blood and pyramids of heads are raised in the important cities. Tamerlane then returns to Samarkand, leaving the Ganges basin utterly devastated and plunged in anarchy. For seven years upheavals shake the country. The governor appointed by Tamerlane founds the Sayyid dynasty. Later on the Lodis, an Afghan dynasty, come to the throne of Delhi (1451-1526). The Lodi rulers erect a series of remarkable tombs in Indo-Persian style. But they soon succumb to a new enemy : Babur.

Babur, intrepid swordsman and Renaissance humanist all in one, was for twelve years king of Fergana. This descendant of Tamerlane and Genghis-Khan dreams of rebuilding his grand-father's empire. He succeeds in taking Samarkand but is soon defeated, ousted from his ancestral dominions and left with only his name and his sword. He takes

The tomb of Isa Khan at Delhi, built on an octagonal plan, dates from 1547. The gallery is buttressed by corner pillars with batter. It is crowned with a dome flanked by secondary "pinnacle turrets". This tomb was intended for a member of the court of Sultan Sher Shah who temporarily ousted Humayun from his ancestral dominions.

Right:
The octagonal gallery with its massive pillars supporting the arcades of the tomb of Isa Khan at Delhi.

refuge in the stronghold of Kabul with the last of his followers. At the head of a small army, he swoops down on the plain of the Ganges through the Khyber pass. At Panipat he puts to flight fifty thousand soldiers and a thousand elephants led by the last Lodi ruler. In 1526, Babur, this fearless and cultured Mongolian, assumes the title of padishah and proclaims himself the first of the Great Moguls.

Persian Roots

During the entire period of the Mogul empire — distinguished by a pomp and splendor never equalled in India — the arts and sciences betray a deep-rooted Persian influence. The Mongolian conquerors, natives of the steppes of Central Asia, were gradually Islamized when they came into contact with Iranian populations in north-eastern Persia. Before pushing their way into India, they assimilated their vassals' artistic traditions and modes of aesthetic expression. Under the Timurids, the cities of Samarkand, Bukhara, Herat and Bactria (Balkh) experience a brilliant cultural development. This first contact with civilization is destined to leave an indelible imprint on the Mongolians. Timurid rulers are enthusiastic patrons of the arts. They support scholars and miniaturists, architects and philosophers. After every raid or conquest, the Mongolians bring to their court intellectuals and artists whose task will be to render the dynasty illustrious.

Babur is succeeded in 1530 by his son Humayun. He too loses his kingdom and goes into exile in Persia. Sher Shah who has dispossessed him governs the country and raises countless public buildings: caravanserais, hospitals and fortresses. In 1555 however, with the support of the Persian army, Humayun wins back his crown. A year later he falls downstairs in his library and dies. His widow, Haji Begum, has a grand mausoleum built him by a Persian architect. The tomb of Humayun is the prototype of a whole series of amazing Mogul tombs.

The mausoleum of Humayun was built by a Persian architect on his widow's request. Under construction from 1557 to 1565, it may be regarded as the prototype of the great Mogul tombs erected in the seventeenth century. The edifice is built on a terrace supported by a series of arcades. The basic plan is a square with bevel angles typical of Timurid constructions in Persia. The tomb is crowned with a white marble dome. The vast proportions introduce an original feature as well as the marble inlays which replace Persian faïence tiles.

Akbar the Great, Founder of an Empire, a Religion and a City

Few names evoke more splendid echoes than the title of Great Mogul. Among the rulers to whom Muslim India owes its splendour, the Great Mogul Akbar is doubtless the one who left the deepest and most lasting mark on the country, thanks to his brilliant qualities as empire-builder, conqueror and politician and his genius for social, religious and artistic unification.

Akbar wished to embody the link between two worlds: Islam and Hinduism. His whole life bears witness to this never abating preoccupation and dream of amalgamating peoples, traditions and beliefs which takes shape when he creates a new capital, Fatehpur Sikri, near Agra, a precious Chandigarh.

Akbar is born in 1542. He comes to the throne of the Mogul empire in 1556, at the age of fourteen. A contemporary of Henri IV, he is a Renaissance conquistador, a founder of cities, a fervent mystic, a poetry

enthusiast and a genuine Machiavelli all in one. His mother's family goes back to Genghis-Khan. By his grand-father Babur of Samarkand, conqueror of India and first of the Great Moguls, he is descended from Tamerlane. This man destined to transform India into a modern centralized State is in fact a Mongolian from the steppes of Central Asia. He unifies the greater part of the subcontinent, from Ghazni and Kabul on the west all the way to the delta of the Ganges on the east, and from the Himalayas to the middle of the Deccan. Bengal, Rajasthan, Kashmir, Punjab, Gujarat, Hindustan, Pakistan and Afghanistan come under his rule. His ancestors conquered Persia before swooping down on the plains of India through the Khyber pass. Persian is therefore spoken at the emperor's court. But Akbar's aim is to further consolidate his empire. He is not long in propagating a common language throughout the whole of India. This language, known as Hindustani, is a mixture of Urdu and Persian, written in Arabic letters.

Though illiterate, having spent his youth on the battlefield, Akbar is interested in the sciences, mathematics, metaphysics and art. He brings together one of the richest libraries in Asia in which we find works in Hindi, Persian, Greek, Arabic etc. He invites writers and scholars to his court and takes pleasure in their conversations.

Towards an Islamo-Hindu Syncretism

But religious problems are unquestionably the most pressing concern of this brilliant statesman, valiant warrior and wise administrator who reorganizes the financial system of the empire, centralizes the administration and consolidates territorial unity. He is well aware that the main obstacle to the cultural and political unification of his possessions consists in the diversity of religious persuasions. His curiosity is probably aroused by the various cults and practices he can observe in his own household. Some of his wives are daughters of Rajput or Parsi princes. The emperor thus comes into contact with Mazdaism and the religious world of India. He even has a temple of fire built in his harem, for he looks upon flame, light and the sun itself as revelations of God.

Brought up in Sunnite orthodoxy, he nonetheless gives ear to the Shiite scholars who propagate the tolerant doctrines of Iranian Islam. He wishes first of all to conciliate the two branches of the Muslim faith. Later on he fathoms Hindu philosophy and dreams of a syncretism unifying Sufism (Muslim mysticism based on sublime speculations in comparison with which ritual obligations and the fear of heresy are but trifling concerns) and the Vishnuist conceptions of pre-Muslim India.

This curiosity gains him the ill will of the ulemas, guardians of the Muslim doctrine. Because of his tolerance, he is called a heretic by those who wish to preserve the Muslim faith free from all outside influence. That need be no obstacle: Akbar is the master. He strips the ulemas of their political and judicial prerogatives and grants vast powers to his own friends, ready to accept a less formalist religion and audacious, innovative speculations.

Founder of a Religion

In the new city which he has created at Fatehpur Sikri, he organizes interdenominational discussions and debates. He invites Buddhists, Hindu wise men, Vishnuists and Shivaists, Zoroastrians and Christians and sets them against the learned men of Sunnite and Shiite Islam. Among the Christians invited to Akbar's court, we should call attention to the presence of three Jesuit Fathers from the Portuguese colony of Goa. One of them, the nephew of the general of the order, Claudio Acquaviva, long believes he will succeed in converting the ruler. He comes to Fatehpur Sikri in 1580 to take part in these meetings which seem to foretell the great modern day ecumenical councils.

In an atmosphere of spiritual anxiety aroused by the belief in the end of the world a thousand years after the coming of the Prophet, according to a millenarian eschatology prevalent among the Shiites who hold the impending return of the Mahdi, twelfth Imam and "Master of Time", to herald the Last Judgment, Akbar founds his own religion, "tauhid-i-ilahi", which conciliates the positive elements of all faiths as he was able to appreciate them in the course of the debates at Fatehpur Sikri. Akbar is the spiritual leader of the faithful, the representative of God on earth. He issues decrees ordering the muezzins to greet the rising sun with the ritual Islamic expression "Allahu akbar". The original meaning of this

Below right:
View of the galleries lining the Diwan-i-Am, or hall of the public audience, at Fatehpur Sikri.

The architecture of Fatehpur Sikri combines Muslim and Hindu features. Here we see stone corbelling modelled after wooden structures peculiar to Indian architecture. The Diwan-i-Khas, built entirely in red sandstone, thus takes on the appearance of a work of carpentry.

Overleaf (p. 72-73):
Courtyard of the mosque at Fatehpur Sikri, built in 1571. On the left, the white marble mausoleum erected in 1580 in homage to the memory of Salim Chishti, a holy man held in reverence by Akbar. In the centre, the great gate, or Buland Derwaze (Gate of Magnificence), built by Akbar after a successful military campaign in the Deccan.

In the interior of Fatehpur Sikri, the Jodh Bai palace appears as a distinct structure cut off from the other edifices on the hillcrest. This is the harem, where Akbar kept some three hundred odalisks. The entrance door ressembles the fortified gates of Mogul cities (1569).

The decoration typical of the edifices built at Fatehpur Sikri has much in common with wood carving. The profuse ornamentation is derived from Hindu temples.

71

Facing page (above):
The eastern gate of the mosque at Fatehpur Sikri, known as the Badshahi Derwaze, or Royal Gate. Akbar came this way when he went to the mosque to pray.

Facing page (below):
The tomb of Salim Chishti at Fatehpur Sikri is surrounded by a ring gallery lined with marble traceried windows This gallery was reserved for the rite of circumambulation performed by the devout around the saintly hermit's tomb.

The great gate known as the Buland Derwaze leads into the Jamma Masjid at Fatehpur Sikri. This arch, 41 m (135 feet) high, is the loftiest one in the whole of Muslim India. It was completed in 1575.

Detail of the delicate marble traceried windows surrounding the tomb of Salim Chishti at Fatehpur Sikri. This stone lace was filed down by craftsmen who were paid in proportion to the amount of powdered marble thus obtained at the end of each day.

verse is "Allah is great", but it may also be understood to proclaim: "Akbar is God!". At the same time, he publishes an edict of tolerance, in 1593, proclaiming all men, Muslims and Hindus, equal in his empire. This decree represents a veritable revolution. It well indicates the broadness of mind characteristic of the activity of this potentate who constantly militates in favour of the abolition of castes, the elimination of all discrimination between Muslim masters and Hindu vanquished, the factual unity of the peoples of India.

Creator of a City

At the age of twenty-three, Akbar has as yet no heir. This is a subject for great anxiety. He resolves to consult Salim Chishti, a famous Muslim hermit who lives at Sikri, about forty kilometres (25 miles) from Agra. The Shaikh promises him a fine healthy son who is born on August 30, 1569 at this remote site where the ruler has sent his wife. Since he has already lost twins, he deems it advisable to put the unborn child under the protection of the wise man. He decides that Sikri will henceforth be the centre of his empire and founds a new city which is christened Fatehpur Sikri, i.e. "Sikri, City of Victory", on account of a victory he has recently gained in Gujarat.

Contrary to his architectural undertakings at Agra, then known as Akbar-Abad, where he has entirely rebuilt the Red Fort and in particular the Jahangri Mahal palace, at Sikri Akbar adopts a new conception of town planning. At Akbar-Abad, the citadel, a crescent-shaped edifice situated on the bank of the Jumna, is rigorously oriented. The directing principle is a chequer-board layout. At Fatehpur Sikri, Akbar decides to break away from these traditional imperatives. He draws a bold plan in which, though the four cardinal points continue to furnish the basic principle of orientation, the topography of the site is also taken into account. The town is built on a ridge running from south-west to north-east. The architectural complexes are therefore disposed along a diagonal. The building line follows the hillcrest. Courtyards are no longer nested one within another or laid out symmetrically on either side of an axis, as it was generally the case in fortified towns. The structures are now staggered according to a subtle, wholly asymmetrical arrangement which opens up original vistas and makes for quite surprising street-crossings.

A New Architecture

The town is surrounded by a wall except on the north-west where the boundary was formed by an artificial lake. It includes an impressive complex of official and administrative buildings: palaces, mosque, audience halls, caravanserais, mint, record office, hospital, harem, baths, playground, ornamental lakes, stables and gardens.

Just as Akbar's conception of town planning breaks away from

traditional practices, his contributions in the field of architecture also represent a new, syncretic style. The forms and techniques in use among Hindu architects are combined with those of the Muslim world. Islamic arches and domes rub shoulders with the corbels and "petrified" timber work typical of the monuments of pre-Muslim India.

Thus for example the ruler makes use of the marble tracery characteristic of Jain temples like those at Mount Abu in the Rajasthan province. These edifices bequeath to following centuries a system of corbels, consoles and braces. Akbar's architects also avail themselves of stone pillars and architraves which represent a transposition of the kind of architectural construction used in primitive Buddhist monasteries built in wood. In architecture, as in religion, the ruler seeks to amalgamate Indian and Muslim traditions.

But the city of Fatehpur Sikri, founded in 1569, is inhabited for only a short time, on account of the lack of drinking water which soon proves to be a serious problem. Indeed, the artificial lake created on the north-west is not long in drying up and the emperor's court returns to Agra (Akbar-Abad). Apart from a brief re-occupation by Sultan Mohammed Shah in the eighteenth century, the buildings of Fatehpur Sikri remain standing empty up to the present day, like a ghost town, haunted by the memory of the brillant and visionary padishah, Akbar the Great.

When Akbar dies in 1605 at the peak of his glory, he has already begun the construction of his mausoleum at Sikandra, near Agra, where a wholly new formula is adopted. This complex, christened Behisht-Abad, the City of Paradise, is built according to a Persian plan known as Chahar Bagh, i.e. four gardens. The four monumental gates leading into these gardens are disposed opposite one another, thus forming the four arms of a cross. In the middle of the cruciform funerary enclosure, an enormous pyramidal edifice with five stories surrounded by galleries, offers once again an amalgamation of arches and domes with the "petrified" tent frames mentioned above.

The southern entrance gate leading to Akbar's tomb at Sikandra, near Agra. The edifice crowned with four minarets encased in white marble was completed by Jahangir in 1613. The red sandstone façades are adorned with sumptuous inlays.

Akbar's mausoleum at Sikandra combines
Muslim arcades with Hindu building
techniques derived from carpentry. The
result is an elaborate, multi-storey surrealistic labyrinth.

At the summit of Akbar's mausoleum is a
vast platform surrounded by a marble gallery. The bounds are marked by traceried
windows characterized by an extraordinary
delicacy of design. In the middle of this esplanade we find the Great Mogul's
cenotaph. The true sarcophagus is hidden
in the heart of the monument.

The upper story, surrounded by a gallery lined with marble traceried windows, encloses a lofty platform. In the middle of this aerial esplanade, we find a white marble cenotaph, replica of the true sarcophagus hidden in the heart of the pyramid. The vault of heaven itself serves as a dome, in accordance with a symbolism often employed in contemporaneous Persian architecture. In the heart of the structure, plunged in gloom, the true sarcophagus bears only one word : "Akbar".

This system of a double burial place, peculiar to the peoples of the steppe, recalls the ruler's Mongolian descent. In accordance with the new religious principles established by the king, the head of the deceased is turned to the east and the rising sun and not towards Mecca and the Kaaba. The entire organization partakes of a complex symbolism based on the contrast between the gloomy abode of the deceased and the paradisiac splendour promised the soul in the empyrean.

The tomb, completed by Jahangir in 1613, well complies with the definition of Mogul architecture given by Reginald Heber in 1849 : "They build like giants but with the precision of jewellers".

The mausoleum of Itimad ud-Daula, "Pillar of State", Jahangir's father-in-law and grand vizier, was erected in 1628 at Agra by his daughter Nur Jahan, "Light of the World". One should take note of the exquisitely designed decoration.

Right:
Mosaics of semi-precious stones decorating panels at the base of Itimad ud-Daula's tomb. The pattern forms a network of intersecting octagons.

Facing page:
The upper pavilion of the tomb of Itimad ud-Daula houses the cenotaphs of the grand vizier and his wife. It is surrounded by remarkable marble traceried windows. A subtle light filters through this lattice-work.

The Splendour of the Mogul Empire

After Akbar's death, the dynasty of the Great Moguls enters into a period of splendour and bloodshed, pomp and horror that recalls at times the atmosphere of Shakespearean tragedies. Rebel princes blinded by their own father, brothers or nephews assassinated by rulers for the slightest suspicion of rivalry, a king who covets his neighbour's wife and does away with his rival, persecutors of Hindus and Christians, incapable drunkards and debauchees cannot succeed in tarnishing the splendour of the masterpieces created during the seventeenth century. Northern India is studded with white marble monuments which give shape to the wildest dreams of the Thousand and One Nights.

Akbar's first born son, Prince Salim, is designated by his father to succeed him on the throne of the Mogul empire. Salim is however an alcoholic who never measures up to the task of governing. In 1605, he

The Taj Mahal in all its splendour. The edifice, under construction from 1632 to 1652, was built at Agra by Shah Jahan for his wife Mumtaz Mahal. It is here seen from the raised ornamental pool in the middle of the Persian garden leading to the mausoleum proper which seems to be a majestic and paradisiac vision. In the middle ground, the linear precision of the canal draws the eye and accentuates the perfect symmetry of the structure, harmoniously flanked by four soaring minarets. Our attention is then attracted by the vast recess, or iwan, with its arch, 20 m (66 feet) high, crowning the door which leads to the cenotaphs of the empress and her husband. The square terrace which serves as a pedestal for the monument and its four minarets is no less than 100 m (330 feet) long on each side and covers an area of one hectare (2.5 acres). The white marble used in construction makes this masterpiece of purity and precision seem almost unreal. Beauty is an obvious fact, crystal clear and seemingly derived from a mathematical formula. Yet this simplicity has not risen unspontaneously. It is the result of subtle geometric combinations and extremely complex optical effects. Thus the hemispherical dome crowning the structure's central hall is hidden beneath a second, bulb-shaped dome, it alone visible from the outside. Between these two shells is an entirely blind, "wasted" space vaster than the hall itself. This is indeed a factitious art with a purely symbolic meaning. The architects who conceived the Taj Mahal wished to create an image of Paradise on earth.

Bulb-shaped dome of the Taj Mahal, seen from the second balcony of the southwestern minaret. The structure's various components are laid out along a diagonal. The two pinnacles flanking the cant-wall lead to an octagonal pavilion crowned with a dome whose proportions set off the enormous main bulb-shaped dome on its cylindrical drum.

The park of the Taj Mahal, laid out after the Persian manner, as seen from the roof of the mausoleum. In the centre we see the raised pool, situated at the intersection of the two axes, and in the background, the entrance gate at the far end of the 300 m (985 feet) long canal.

Facing page (below):
West of the Taj Mahal, the red sandstone funerary mosque crowned with three white marble domes. This mosque intended for services honouring the memory of the deceased is in its own right one of the gems of Mogul architecture. Nevertheless it is quite overshadowed by the splendour of the central monument. On the right, an elegant summerhouse overlooking the bank of the Jumna.

assumes the name of Jahangir Nur ud-Din, i.e. "Conqueror of the World — Light of the Faith". He marries Nur Mahal ("Light of the Palace"), after having done away with her husband. He soon hands the reins of government over to his wife. The empress changes her name to Nur Jahan, "Light of the World", and appoints her father, a Persian adventurer going by the name of Mirza Ghias Begh, treasurer and grand vizier of the realm, under the name of Itimad ud-Daula, "Pillar of State".

During the reign of Jahangir, the art of Mogul miniature painting reaches its peak. The basic pictorial vocabulary is quite close to that we remark in Persian works executed during the Timurid period. However the style has now become sharper and clearer. Debauchee though he may be, Jahangir is nonetheless a patron of the arts. He completes Akbar's mausoleum at Sikandra and places unlimited funds at his wife's disposal for the construction of Itimad ud-Daula's tomb at Agra. This tomb is one of the wonders of Jahangir's reign, in spite of its relatively small dimensions, due to the fact that the deceased was not of royal descent.

The formula here chosen, with its "pinnacle turrets" at the four corners of the structure and the upper chamber housing the cenotaph built in the shape of a pavilion entirely surrounded by finely chiselled marble traceried bay windows, unites several conspicuous features of Akbar's monument: the four minaret-like gates and raised central esplanade. The structure's basic plan is a square centred round two lines meeting at right angles like the walks which divide the park into four gardens in accordance with the Persian layout already seen at Sikandra.

Shah Jahan at the Height of his Glory

In 1612, Prince Khurram, destined to rule as the fourth Great Mogul under the name of Shah Jahan, marries Mumtaz Mahal, grand-daughter of Itimad ud-Daula. He succeeds Jahangir in 1628. Unlike Akbar, he favours a policy of religious intolerance: he sets fire to the Portuguese trading stations at Goa and takes the Jesuit Fathers prisoner. He humiliates the Hindus, although his own mother practiced the Hindu religion...

Like his predecessor, he rules jointly with his wife. The empress Mumtaz Mahal accompanies him even on his military campaigns. When she dies in childbirth in 1630; he decrees two years of mourning at court, takes less and less interest in public matters and seems about to drop the reins of government. He is so deeply affected that he even thinks of abdicating. He finally gives up this idea and applies himself to the task of immortalizing the memory of his beloved wife. For her, he devotes his energy to the construction of an admirable mausoleum — the most perfect tomb in the world — the Taj Mahal at Agra. This task demands twenty years. The tomb begun in 1632 is completed in 1652.

He also undertakes the erection of the Jamma Masjid, or Friday Mosque, at Delhi, the largest mosque in India. As in the Taj Mahal, Mogul style here attains an unmatched poise. The edifice is under construction from 1644 to 1658. But Shah Jahan's building fever does not abate for all that. In 1645, he begins to rebuild from top to bottom the Red Fort at Delhi where he dispatches affairs of State when he cannot delegate his powers. This complex begun under Humayun, like that at Agra owes its name to the red sandstone employed for the enclosure wall and defence works. Last but not least, in 1646 he builds the famous Moti Masjid, or Pearl Mosque, at Agra which ranks among the purest creations in Mogul architecture.

After a several year long attempt to drown his sorrows, he falls ill. He has already entrusted his sons with the administration of the various provinces of his empire. In 1658, a struggle for power takes place between his sons. The victor is Aurangzeb. He deludes his father and

View of the façade of the Taj Mahal from the second balcony of the southeastern minaret. In the background, the domes of the funerary mosque.

succeeds in imprisoning him in the palace of the Red Fort at Agra. From the windows of his golden cage, the dethroned king can contemplate the haughty silhouette of the Taj Mahal on the horizon which brings back memories of Mumtaz Mahal. We know that he was planning to construct an identical mausoleum, entirely in black marble, for himself, on the other bank of the Jumna. When Shah Jahan dies after eight years of captivity, his son Aurangzeb refuses to raise this companion tomb and has the deceased ruler interred with his beloved wife in the crypt of the Taj Mahal.

A Symphony in White Marble

In the case of the Taj Mahal, the architectural vocabulary of Mogul India once again appeals to its Persian prototypes. Indeed, a good many Persian mausoleums foretell the formula here chosen : a square structure with bevelled edges, crowned with a horseshoe dome. As in Timurid constructions, the four façades consist in wide, typically Iranian recesses known as iwans. The novelty here resides essentially in the proportions

Apartments of the palace erected in the Red Fort at Agra. Shah Jahan, imprisoned here by his son Aurangzeb, could gaze on the Taj Mahal rising up on the horizon and bringing back memories of his beloved wife Mumtaz Mahal. These marble galleries and open halls look out on the bank of the Jumna.

Right :
Façade of the famous Pearl Mosque at Agra, with its seven arches, three bulb-shaped domes and typically Indian "pinnacle turrets". This place of prayer, built after the Persian manner around a court-yard with a central pool, is the work of Shah Jahan. Construction was begun in 1646.

Above:
View of the façade of the Pearl Mosque at Agra as seen from the northern cloister. We well remark the splendour of this white marble creation with its sharp and graceful outline and exquisite delicacy of design.

which give the central element of the Taj Mahal a haughty dignity, a placid splendour and a crystalline purity. The four disengaged minarets situated on the diagonals of the main building also contribute to the structure's originality. The minarets here mark the corners of the vast terrace which serves as a foundation for the entire complex. Indeed, a similar arrangement was already employed for Jahangir's mausoleum at Lahore. At Lahore, however, the minarets are the essential and by no means a mere frame for a central monument there well nigh non-existent. Jahangir's tiny cenotaph gives the four minarets a claim to consideration wholly lacking at the Taj Mahal where they simply accentuate the symmetry characterizing the edifice.

With its four 45 m (148 feet) high minarets and the dome which rises up to a height of 70 m (230 feet), the Taj Mahal, offering the same strictly symmetrical appearance on all sides, when bathed in sunlight puts on a quite fascinating light show. The white marble façades reflect now pink now bluish hues mirrored in the waters of the central pond or the vast 300 m (985 feet) long canal dominating the grandiose vista which opens out before our eyes when we stand at the entrance gate.

Secluded in the Red Fort at Delhi

Aurangzeb who, like his father, has had all the pretenders to the throne put to death, rules over an empire stretching from Kabul to Madras. He turns out a bigot, opts for strict Sunnite orthodoxy wholly founded on Koranic law, excludes all Hindus from public office and forms a new government of religious fanatics. Aware of the enmity he thus arouses among his subjects, he fears even to cross the gardens between his palace and the Jamma Masjid, situated opposite the Red Fort at Delhi. He decides to have a small private shrine built in the heart of this admirable complex erected by his predecessor following a rigorous plan. The result is the Moti Masjid, or Pearl Mosque, a royal chapel decorated with white marble and crowned with three bulb-shaped domes.

Below:
The Jamma Masjid at Delhi, the largest Muslim sanctuary in India, was erected by Shah Jahan in 1644. It is built in red sandstone and white marble. The sanctuary juts out into an immense cloistered courtyard.

Interior of a pavilion in the Red Fort at Delhi looking out on the Jumna. The delicate traceried windows contrived in monolithic slabs of marble are an example of a technique often used in Mogul architecture to bring cool breezes into the palatial dwellings.

The small Pearl Mosque is a private shrine built in the heart of the Red Fort at Delhi by the bigot Aurangzeb in 1699. The somewhat affected style betrays the decadence of Mogul art.

Portico of the Diwan-i-Khas, or hall of the private audience, in the Red Fort at Delhi. One should take note of the exquisite decoration: inlaid semi-precious stones and acanthus moulding running around the bases and abaci of the pillars. In the background, the Pearl Mosque with its three bulb-shaped domes stands out against a red sandstone wall.

The Maharajahs of Amber and Jaipur

Rajput palaces overlooking the gorges of Amber in the Rajasthan province. A massive fortress towers above the enclosure. These edifices were built by Maharajah Jai Singh I in the seventeenth century. This complex erected on a fortified hilltop protected by walls plunging steeply into the waters of an artificial pool copies the layout of Mogul palaces at Delhi and Agra.

Below right:
Ceiling of the Jasha Mandir, or "Hall of Glory", entirely lined with mirrors. The palace at Amber is, in all respects; a sumptuous echo of Persian palaces at Isfahan.

The Mongolians have no sooner gained their first victory at Panipat than the Hindu princes of Amber and the Rajasthan province throw in their lot with the invaders. Their destiny is associated with the rise of the Great Mogul dynasty. The daughter of one of these Rajput maharajahs marries Akbar in order to ratify the alliance. Entrenched in their eagle's nest at Amber, situated on the road to Delhi like a fortified robbers' lair commanding a narrow gorge, the Rajputs assume dominion over a vast territory. They raise regiments of proud warriors and support the campaigns of the Mogul emperors in the southern regions of the Deccan.

As concrete proof of the Rajput success, Jai Singh I erects in the seventeenth century a sumptuous palace within the walls of the fort of Amber complete with refined state apartments, gardens laid out after the Mogul manner and audience halls entirely lined with mirrors such as the Jasha Mandir, or "Hall of Glory", and the Shish Mahal, or "Palace of Mirrors". This architecture calls to mind the Mogul constructions at Delhi and Agra. A certain taste for prolixity, superabundant details and outright ostentation seems to draw inspiration from Hindu traditions though also in keeping with the style in vogue in Persian palaces.

In the eighteenth century, Jai Singh II who rules from 1699 to 1743 undertakes to erect a new capital in the plain at the mouth of the gorge of Amber. This new city will be christened Jaipur. It is surrounded by walls and differs from most Indian urban centres in as much as the basic plan is a chequer-board layout. This complex dating from 1727 has probably come under the influence of Mogul palace districts. The layout of the town centre is more or less an exact copy of the Red Fort at Delhi with it's various palatial edifices. We find here a Diwan-i-Am, or hall of the public audience, a Diwan-i-Khas, or hall of the private audience, and countless miniature canals running through the inner

The pomp of the Rajput maharajahs of Amber is particularly conspicuous in the Shish Mahal, or "Palace of Mirrors", which was Jai Singh I's hall of the private audience. Here too the ornamentation is derived from Safavid Persia.

The gorges of Amber which command the road to Delhi, here viewed from the palace roofs. In the foreground, courtyards and gardens within the enceinte.

In the city of Jaipur, built in the early eighteenth century by Jai Singh II at the mouth of the gorge of Amber, the astonishing Palace of Winds, or Hawa Mahal, is a late (1799) but quite charming work of architecture. This façade with its countless loggias and delicate traceried windows is characteristic of late Mogul art. Tradional decorative features have now become baroque and extravagant.

The astronomical observatory, or Jantar Mantar, at Jaipur, built by Maharajah Jai Singh II in 1728, houses a series of masonry instruments devised to study movements of celestial bodies. They are enlarged copies of manual devices such as astrolabes, sextants and theodolites.

chambers and gardens. It was in fact the usual practice for provincial lords to copy the layout of the palaces built for the Great Moguls. When Mogul power begins to wane, the maharajahs continue to construct palace complexes which may be called genuine "images of Paradise". This will to create a paradisiac setting appears quite clearly at Delhi, where Shah Jahan has the following verse graven on a wall of his hall of the private audience :

"If Paradise exists on earth,
It is here, it is here, it is here !"

Besides these courtly riches, the city of Jaipur includes, in the very heart of the palace complex, an extraordinary astronomical observatory, or Jantar Mantar. Jai Singh II has these peculiar stellar measuring instruments constructed at Delhi, Mathura, Ujjin and Benares, as well as at Jaipur. The observatory at Jaipur, under construction from 1728 to 1733, is, relatively speaking, a model of perfection. It houses a gigantic triangular gnomon 30 m (100 feet) high, sighting gear, or rachides, devised to determine and measure location and movements of visible celestial bodies, enormous copper machines and underground constructions with chambers and passageways cut out for the astronomers.

Actually, the aim was to obtain more accurate measurements than those furnished by the manual devices in use up to that time. And the means chosen to this end was the construction of a set of instruments a hundred times larger than anything seen before. The result is an astonishing and seemingly surrealistic architecture. Its pure and geometrically functionnal forms (circles, cylinders, hollow hemispheres, triangles, arcs in the plane of the ecliptic, etc.) have given birth to a decidedly modern work of architecture.

Indo-Islamic art, adapting Mogul forms and techniques to astronomical imperatives, has thus created, to delight a cultured Hindu maharajah living in the Age of Enlightenment, the most extravagant construction imaginable — at the same time a hymn to science.

The observatory at Jaipur includes a series of rachides, devices employed for determining the position of stars in relation to the ecliptic. The scale of measure is graven on circular marble surfaces perpendicular to the line of sight.

Conclusion

Such then is this land of India, manifold and baffling, India with its thousand gods and deep thinkers, its complex rites and its philosophers preoccupied with the soul's destiny, the abolition of desire and the alleviating of suffering, India whose poets have conceived in Sanskrit inspired hymns such as the Upanishads to say nothing of the great epic poems known as the Mahabharata and the Ramayana, India which has raised its admirable temples like a lyric hymn to glorify its gods and erected in honour of its rulers the most perfect mausoleums in the history of mankind...

India is the home of lofty spiritual yearnings, a land which has given birth to a profusion of philosophies baffling the western mind. It is a continent where 130 languages and 1600 dialects are spoken, a country where the multitude of sects and religions rubbing shoulders bears

The giant triangular gnomon of the observatory at Jaipur reaches a height of 30 m (98 feet) and is in itself a genuine edifice with inner stairways and chambers for the astronomers. What surprises us the most, however, is the curved marble surface which ressembles a modern abstract sculpture.

The "surrealistic" structures of the observatory at Jaipur, like Mogul architecture at Delhi and Agra, are executed in red sandstone and white marble with here and there a touch of stucco.

witness to a never abating quest of remedies for the rigours of the human condition. It is the birthplace of Buddhism, a religion which conquered Southeast Asia after having almost entirely disappeared in its native land, but furnished both China and Japan with their masterpieces.

Last but not least, we should not forget that one of mankind's most important scientific discoveries has its origins in India : the invention of the number zero, without which modern mathematics would be wholly inconceivable. This precious zero made its way to the West via the Arab lands and marked the beginning of the scientific era. It seems indeed a bit disconcerting that India with its time-honoured traditions is the birthplace not only of impressive religious systems (yoga being the last avatar exported to our own hectic civilizations) but also of a fundamental scientific notion which still stimulates modern thought.

Such then are the hidden treasures of the world of India.

The rachides at Jaipur rise up to heaven like a launching pad for interstallar spaceships, the scenery of a science fiction play or a hymn to science. This "folly" of a Hindu maharajah who lived during the Mogul period bears witness to the premonitory curiosity of the great Rajput noblemen and their desire for knowledge.

Photo credits

The 150 colour photographs that illustrate this work devoted to "The World of India" were all provided by Henri Stierlin, Geneva, except for the following documents:

    Maurice Babey, Basle (Ziolo, Paris), , p. 24, 25
    Yvan Butler, Geneva, p. 61,
    Jean Mohr, Geneva, p. 62, 63, 64,
    Nicolas Bouvier, Geneva, p. 78, 79.

The author and photographer is most grateful to the Indian authorities and in particular to the Board of Tourism and Air India for the cordial assistance given him during his expeditions in India.